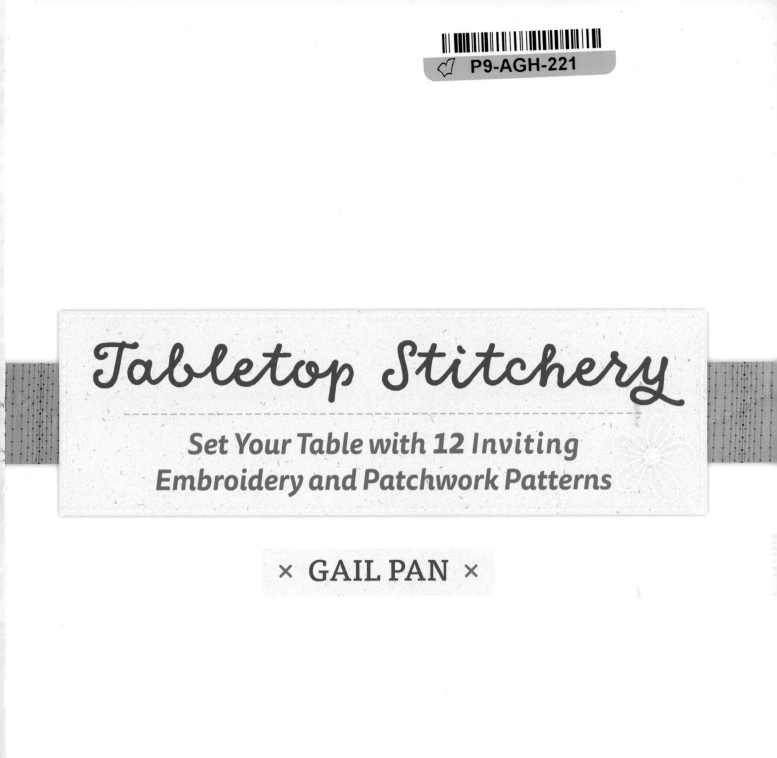

Tabletop Stitchery

Set Your Table with 12 Inviting Embroidery and Patchwork Patterns

× GAIL PAN ×

Martingale®
Create with Confidence

WITHDRAWN

Tabletop Stitchery
Set Your Table with 12 Inviting Embroidery
and Patchwork Patterns
© 2021 by Gail Pan

Martingale®
18939 120th Ave NE, Suite 101
Bothell, WA 98011-9511 USA
ShopMartingale.com

Printed in Hong Kong
26 25 24 23 22 21   8 7 6 5 4 3 2 1

Library of Congress Cataloging-in-Publication Data is available upon request.

ISBN: 978-1-68356-160-6

MISSION STATEMENT

We empower makers who use fabric and yarn
to make life more enjoyable.

CREDITS

PUBLISHER AND
CHIEF VISIONARY OFFICER
Jennifer Erbe Keltner

CONTENT DIRECTOR
Karen Costello Soltys

DESIGN MANAGER
Adrienne Smitke

TECHNICAL EDITOR
Nancy Mahoney

PRODUCTION MANAGER
Regina Girard

COPY EDITOR
Sheila Chapman Ryan

PHOTOGRAPHER
Brent Kane

ILLUSTRATOR
Sandy Loi

Contents

Introduction

I'm Gail Pan, an embroiderer and quilter from Australia, and I love stitching! I enjoy spending time with friends or at home, stitching and sewing lots of different things. I especially love decorating my home with table runners and toppers. Handmade toppers fill your home with flowers, birds, and baskets. Toppers can also help you celebrate holidays and seasons like Christmas and springtime.

Whether you're an experienced embroiderer or a beginner, you'll find projects in this book that are a great way to have fun with embroidery. If you need a bit more information about embroidery, you'll find it in "General Instructions" on page 44. Whatever your experience level, enjoy making the designs and have fun on your stitching journey!

Pretty in Blue

A basket of cheerful blue flowers is sure to brighten your table and your day.

Materials

Yardage is based on 42"-wide fabric. Fat quarters measure 18" × 21".

- ✖ 1 fat quarter of white tone on tone for embroidery background
- ✖ ¼ yard of blue print for setting rectangles
- ✖ ¼ yard of navy solid for binding
- ✖ ½ yard of fabric for backing
- ✖ 14" × 35" piece of batting
- ✖ 1 skein *each* of 6-strand embroidery floss in variegated light blue, variegated medium blue, dark blue, medium blue, and light blue
- ✖ White pearl cotton, size 8, for quilting
- ✖ ⅓ yard of lightweight fusible interfacing, 18" to 20" wide, for stabilizing embroidery
- ✖ 1¾ yards of ¾"-wide cream lace
- ✖ Brown Pigma pen
- ✖ Appliqué or quilter's glue

Cutting

All measurements include ¼" seam allowances.

From the white tone on tone, cut:
1 strip, 10" × 21"; crosscut into:
    1 piece, 7" × 10"
    2 pieces, 4" × 10"

From the lightweight fusible interfacing, cut:
1 piece, 7" × 10"
2 pieces, 4" × 10"

From the blue print, cut:
1 strip, 6½" × 42"; crosscut into:
    2 pieces, 6½" × 9½"
    2 pieces, 3½" × 9½"

From the navy solid, cut:
3 strips, 1½" × 42"

Embroidering the Designs

1. Using the patterns (page 9) and the Pigma pen, trace the basket design onto the right side of the white 7" × 10" piece. Trace the row of flowers onto the right side of each white 4" × 10" piece. Fuse the interfacing to the back of the marked pieces.

2. Using two strands of floss, stitch the designs following the embroidery key on the pattern. Press.

✖ 7

Assembling the Runner

Press seam allowances in the directions indicated by the arrows.

1. Centering the embroidery, trim the embroidered basket piece to 6½" × 9½". Trim each of the embroidered flowers pieces to 3½" × 9½".

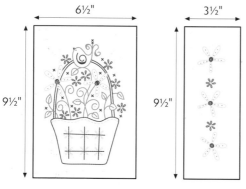

Embroidery placement

2. Referring to the runner assembly diagram below, lay out the blue 3½" × 9½" pieces, the blue 6½" × 9½" pieces, and the embroidered basket and flowers pieces in a row. Join the pieces. The runner top should measure 30½" × 9½".

Quilting and Finishing

1. Layer the runner top, batting, and backing; baste. Using the white pearl cotton and big-stitch quilting (page 46), quilt a wavy line vertically through the middle of the smaller blue pieces and two wavy lines through the larger blue pieces.

2. Cut six 9½"-long pieces of lace. Glue baste a piece of lace on each seamline, with the scallops facing away from the embroidered pieces. Use a running stitch and medium blue floss to secure the lace.

3. Use the navy 1½"-wide strips to make single-fold binding and then attach the binding to the runner (page 47).

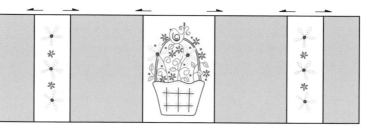

Runner assembly

Embroidery Key

—————— Backstitch

⬤ Backstitch to fill between lines

✕ Cross-stitch

• French knot

⌒ Lazy daisy

- - - - - Running stitch

Fields of Flowers

Stitch a row of whimsical flowers for each side of this topper so you can enjoy them no matter which side of the table you're seated on.

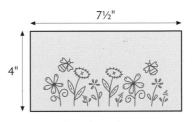

FINISHED TABLE MAT: 20½" × 20½"

Materials

Yardage is based on 42"-wide fabric. Fat quarters measure 18" × 21".

* ¼ yard *OR* 1 fat quarter of cream tone on tone for embroidery background
* 1 fat quarter of pink print for blocks and binding
* ¼ yard of red dot for sashing and border
* ¾ yard of fabric for backing
* 25" × 25" piece of batting
* 1 skein of 6-strand embroidery floss in variegated pink-and-brown
* Ecru pearl cotton, size 8, for quilting
* ⅓ yard of lightweight fusible interfacing, 18" to 20" wide, for stabilizing embroidery
* Brown Pigma pen
* ¼" quilter's tape (optional; see page 46)

Cutting

All measurements include ¼" seam allowances.

From the cream tone on tone cut:
1 strip, 5" × 42"; crosscut into 4 pieces, 5" × 8½"

From the lightweight fusible interfacing, cut:
4 pieces, 5" × 8½"

From the pink print, cut:
5 strips, 1½" × 21"
1 square, 7½" × 7½"
4 squares, 4" × 4"

From the red dot, cut:
2 strips, 2½" × 42"; crosscut into:
    2 strips, 2½" × 16½"
    2 strips, 2½" × 20½"
2 strips, 1½" × 42"; crosscut into:
    2 strips, 1½" × 16½"
    2 strips, 1½" × 7½"
    4 strips, 1½" × 4"

Embroidering the Designs

1. Using the pattern (page 13) and the Pigma pen, trace the embroidery design onto the right side of each cream piece. Fuse the interfacing to the backs of the marked pieces.

2. Using two strands of floss, stitch the designs following the embroidery key on the pattern. Press.

3. Centering the embroidery, trim the embroidered pieces to 4" × 7½".

7½"

4"

Embroidery placement

Assembling the Table Mat

Press seam allowances in the directions indicated by the arrows.

1. Join two pink 4" squares, two red 1½" × 4" strips, and one embroidered piece to make a side row. Make two rows measuring 4" × 16½", including seam allowances.

Make 2 side rows,
4" × 16½".

2. Join two embroidered pieces, the two red 1½" × 7½" strips, and the pink 7½" square, making sure the flowers face inward. The center row should measure 7½" × 16½", including seam allowances.

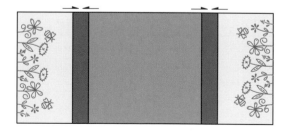

Make 1 center row,
7½" × 16½".

3. Join the side rows, red 1½" × 16½" strips, and the center row as shown. The table-mat center should measure 16½" square, including seam allowances.

Table-mat assembly

4. Sew the red 2½" × 16½" strips to opposite sides of the table mat. Sew the red 2½" × 20½" strips to the top and bottom edges to complete the table mat. Press seam allowances toward the borders. The table mat should measure 20½" square.

Quilting and Finishing

1. Layer the table-mat top, batting, and backing; baste. Using the ecru pearl cotton, quilter's tape, and big-stitch quilting (page 46), quilt through the middle of each sashing strip. Quilt a wavy line in the middle of each border strip. Stitch two wavy lines through each pink square diagonally from corner to corner.

2. Use the pink 1½"-wide strips to make single-fold binding and then attach the binding to the table mat (page 47).

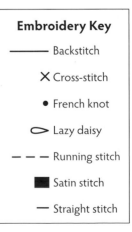

Embroidery Key

——— Backstitch

✕ Cross-stitch

• French knot

⌒ Lazy daisy

– – – Running stitch

■ Satin stitch

— Straight stitch

Dainty Doilies

Cute little doilies are perfect resting spots for small vases of flowers or a special collection. Turn the page for more seasonal motifs.

✕ FINISHED DOILY: 8½" diameter ✕

Materials for 1 Doily

- ✻ 1 square, 10" × 10", of cream tone on tone for embroidery background
- ✻ 1 square, 10" × 10", of lightweight fusible interfacing for stabilizing embroidery
- ✻ 1 square, 10" × 10", of backing fabric
- ✻ Brown Pigma pen

Floral Doily

- ✻ 1 skein of plum variegated floss *OR* 1 skein *each* of 6-strand embroidery floss in red, blue, light blue, dark green, light green, olive green, and pink. (The multicolored option is shown on page 16.)
- ✻ 30" of ⅝"-wide cream lace

Reindeer Doily

- ✻ Pearl cotton, size 12, in variegated red, variegated green, brown, and yellow
- ✻ 30" of ½"-wide red rickrack

Pumpkin Doily

- ✻ Pearl cotton, size 12, in variegated green and variegated orange
- ✻ 30" of ½"-wide cream rickrack

Bird Doily

- ✻ Pearl cotton, size 12, in variegated green, variegated blue, and variegated red
- ✻ 30" of ⅝"-wide cream lace

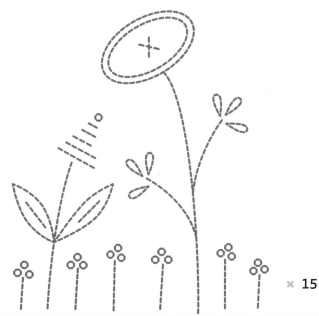

Embroidering the Design

1. Using the Pigma pen, trace the half-circle pattern (page 18) onto the right side of the cream square, making sure to trace the inner and outer lines. Flip the half-circle over, matching the ends of the lines, and trace both lines to complete the circle. Trace one of the embroidery patterns (pages 18 and 19) inside the inner circle. You can trace the design just once or at all four creases. Fuse the interfacing square to the wrong side of the marked square.

2. Using two strands of floss or one strand of pearl cotton, embroider the designs following the embroidery key and referring to the photos on page 16. Press.

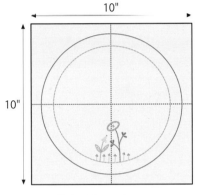

Embroidery placement

Assembling the Doily

1. For the floral and bird doilies, baste the lace onto the right side of the square, with the flat edge of the lace on the marked outer line and the scallops facing inward. For the reindeer and pumpkin doilies, baste the rickrack onto the right side of the square, with the outer edge of the rickrack on the marked outer line. Machine stitch the lace or rickrack in place using a ¼" seam allowance.

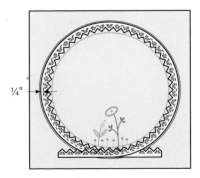

✕ Adjust the Width ✕

If you want less rickrack showing around the edge (as in the pumpkin doily), place the edge of the rickrack outside the marked line.

2. Layer the embroidered top and backing square right sides together and sew on the previously stitched line, leaving a 2" opening for turning. Trim ¼" from the stitched line. Turn the doily right side out through the opening; press well. Hand sew the opening closed and press again.

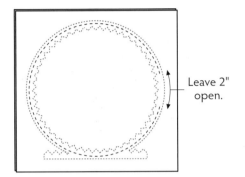

Leave 2" open.

✕ Edging Options ✕

- ✕ *Embellish the edge of the doily with lace (page 16, upper left).*

- ✕ *Allow more of the rickrack to show (page 16, upper right).*

- ✕ *Show just the outer bumps of the rickrack (page 16, lower left).*

- ✕ *Instead of basting the lace in place on the embroidered square, sew the embroidered front and backing together. Turn the doily right side out and then hand stitch the lace around the perimeter of the doily.*

- ✕ *Trace four embroidery patterns around the circle as shown on page 14.*

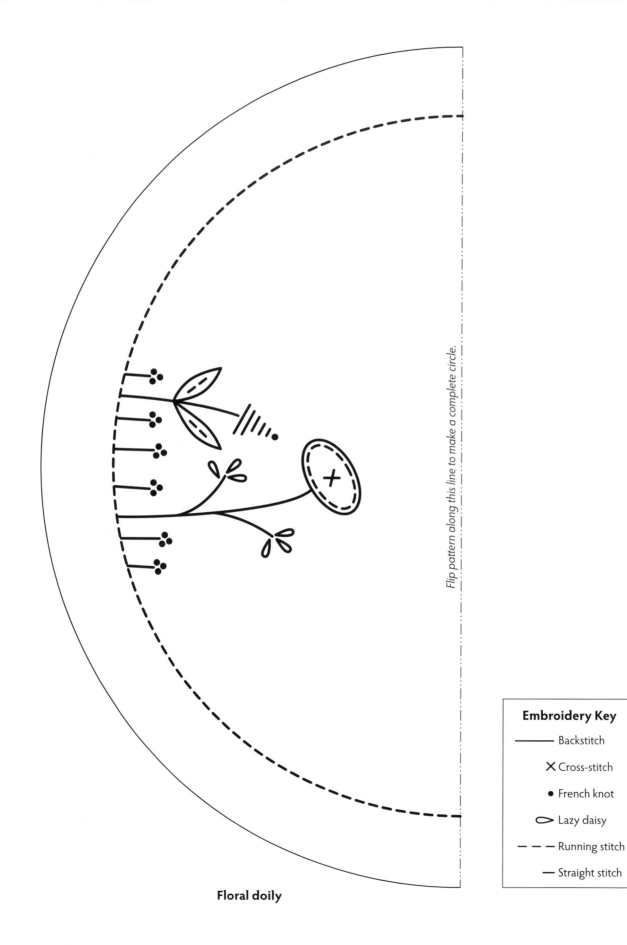

Floral doily

Embroidery Key

——	Backstitch
✕	Cross-stitch
•	French knot
⬭	Lazy daisy
– – –	Running stitch
—	Straight stitch

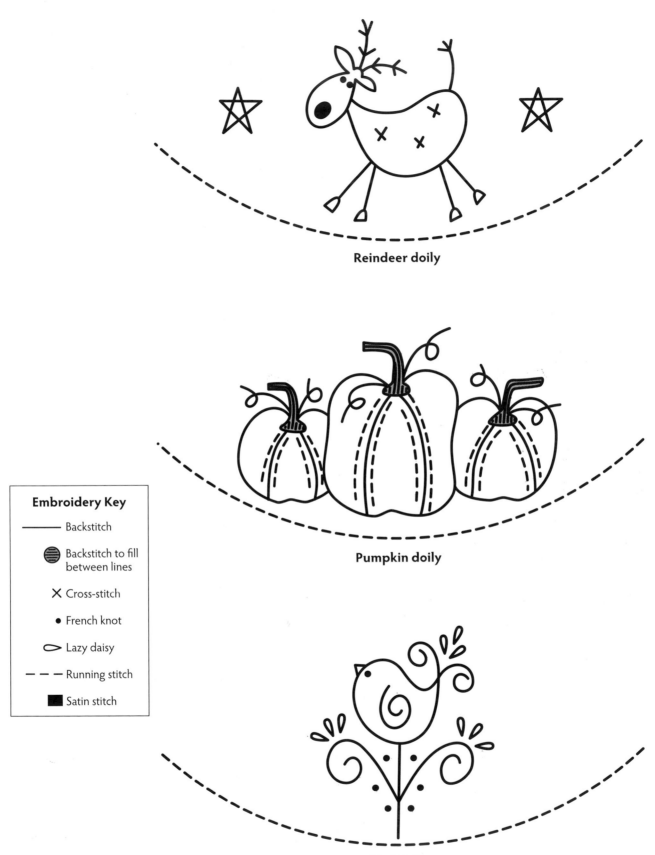

Reindeer doily

Pumpkin doily

Bird doily

Embroidery Key

——— Backstitch

Backstitch to fill between lines

✗ Cross-stitch

• French knot

◯ Lazy daisy

– – – Running stitch

■ Satin stitch

Little Red Cottage

A welcoming table runner is just right for a housewarming gift—or to make your own home more cozy.

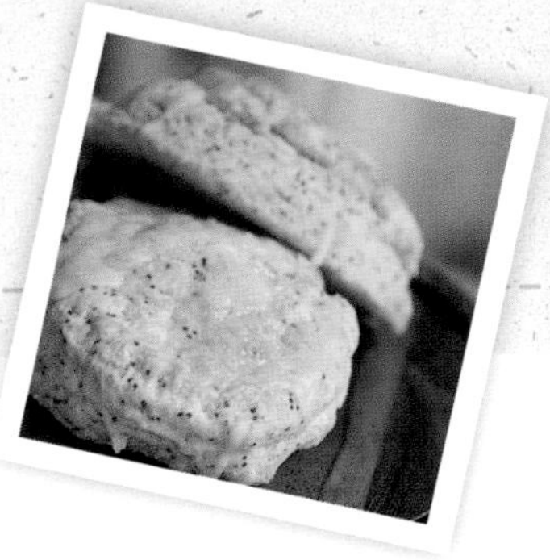

FINISHED TABLE RUNNER: 33½" × 14½"

Materials

Yardage is based on 42"-wide fabric.

- ⅜ yard of cream check for embroidery background
- ½ yard of red print for border and binding
- ⅝ yard of fabric for backing
- 19" × 38" piece of batting
- Variegated red pearl cotton, size 12, for embroidery
- Ecru pearl cotton, size 8, for quilting
- 1 yard of lightweight fusible interfacing, 18" to 20" wide, for stabilizing embroidery
- Brown Pigma pen
- ¼" quilter's tape (optional; see page 46)

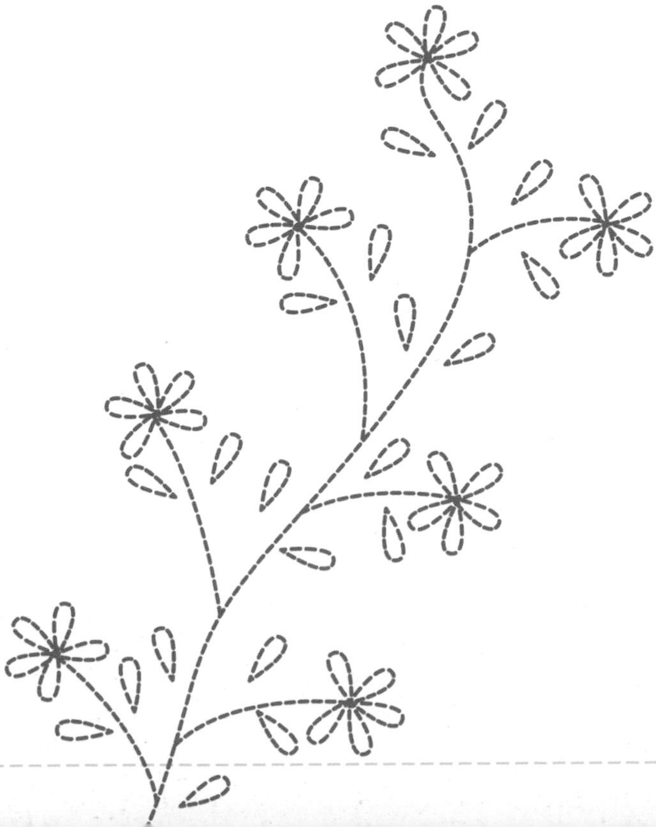

Cutting

All measurements include ¼" seam allowances.

From the cream check, cut:
1 strip, 11" × 30"

From the lightweight fusible interfacing, cut:
1 strip, 11" × 30"

From the red print, cut:
6 strips, 2½" × 42"; crosscut *3 of the strips* into:
- 2 strips, 2½" × 30½"
- 2 strips, 2½" × 11½"
- 4 strips, 2½" × 6½"

Embroidering the Designs

1. Using a Pigma pen, trace the embroidery design (page 23) onto each end of the right side of the cream strip, placing the bottom of the heart 1" from the raw edges and centering the design from side to side. Fuse the interfacing to the wrong side of the marked strip.

2. Using one strand of pearl cotton, embroider the design following the embroidery key on the pattern. Press the completed embroidery from the wrong side.

3. Centering the embroidery, trim the embroidered rectangle to 10½" × 29½".

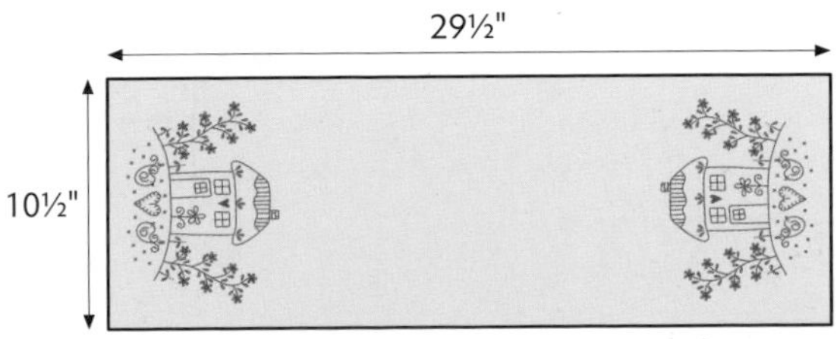

Embroidery placement

Assembling the Runner

Press seam allowances in the directions indicated by the arrows.

1. On one corner of the embroidered strip, make marks 4½" up and 2½" in from the corner. Draw a line between the marks and trim on the line. Repeat to mark and trim the remaining three corners.

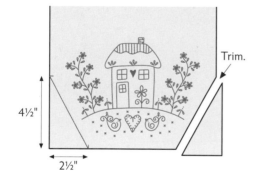

2. Sew a red 2½" × 6½" strip to each diagonal side. Sew a red 2½" × 11½" strip to each short end. Sew a red 2½" × 30½" strip to each long side. Use a rotary

cutter and ruler to trim the ends after each piece is sewn, aligning the ruler with the outer side and diagonal edges.

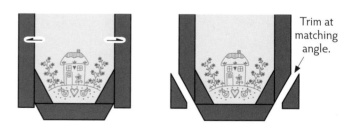

Trim.

Trim at matching angle.

Trim at matching angle.

Quilting and Finishing

Attaching the binding before quilting will make it easier to quilt ¼" from the outer edge of the border.

1. Layer the runner top, batting, and backing; baste. Using the ecru pearl cotton, quilter's tape, and big-stitch quilting (page 46), quilt ¼" from the inner and outer edges of the border. Quilt a diagonal grid in the center of the runner.

2. Use the remaining red 2½"-wide strips to make double-fold binding and then attach the binding to the runner (page 47).

Embroidery Key

— Backstitch

⊤⊤⊤⊤⊤ Blanket stitch

✗ Cross-stitch

• French knot

◯ Lazy daisy

■ Satin stitch

Spring in the Air

Simple hexagons with a touch of embroidery adorn this whimsical table runner.

FINISHED TABLE RUNNER: 28" × 11"

Materials

Yardage is based on 42"-wide fabric.

- ⅜ yard of cream tone on tone for background
- ¼ yard of chartreuse print for hexagon and binding
- 1 piece, 6" × 10" *each*, of red and blue prints for hexagons
- ½ yard of fabric for backing
- 15" × 32" piece of batting
- 1 skein *each* of 6-strand embroidery floss in red, dark blue, light blue, yellow, green, olive green, pink, and variegated green
- ⅞ yard of lightweight fusible interfacing, 18" to 20" wide, for stabilizing embroidery
- Brown Pigma pen
- Cardstock or 2¼" precut hexagons
- Appliqué or quilter's glue (optional)

Cutting

All measurements include ¼" seam allowances.

From the cream tone on tone, cut:
1 strip, 11" × 28"

From the lightweight fusible interfacing, cut:
1 strip, 11" × 28"

From the chartreuse print, cut:
1 piece, 5" × 6"
3 strips, 2½" × 32"

From *each* of the red and blue prints, cut:
2 strips, 5" × 6" (4 total)

Making the Hexagons

1. Using the hexagon pattern (page 27), trace five hexagons onto cardstock. Cut out the hexagons directly on the line. If you're using precut hexagons, skip this step.

2. Place a paper hexagon on the wrong side of each red, blue, and chartreuse piece. Trim the excess fabric, adding a ½" seam allowance all around the paper hexagon.

3. Fold the seam allowances over the paper and baste in place with thread or fabric glue. Press each hexagon well.

4. Whipstitch the hexagons together end to end, placing the chartreuse hexagon in the center. Press well, remove the papers, and press again.

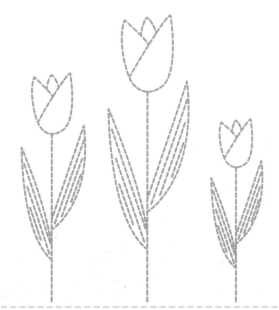

Embroidering the Designs

1. Glue or thread baste the hexagon strip in the center of the cream strip. Hand sew the strip in place using small stitches.

2. Use the Pigma pen to trace the embroidery designs (page 27) onto the right side of the cream strip. Fuse the interfacing strip to the wrong side of the fabric.

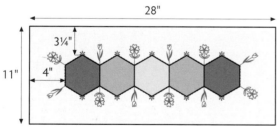

Embroidery placement

3. Using two strands of floss, embroider the designs following the embroidery key and referring to the photo above. Press.

Quilting and Finishing

1. Layer the runner top, batting, and backing; baste. Machine quilt a meandering design around the hexagons and embroidery.

2. Use the chartreuse 2½"-wide strips to make double-fold binding and then attach the binding to the runner (page 47).

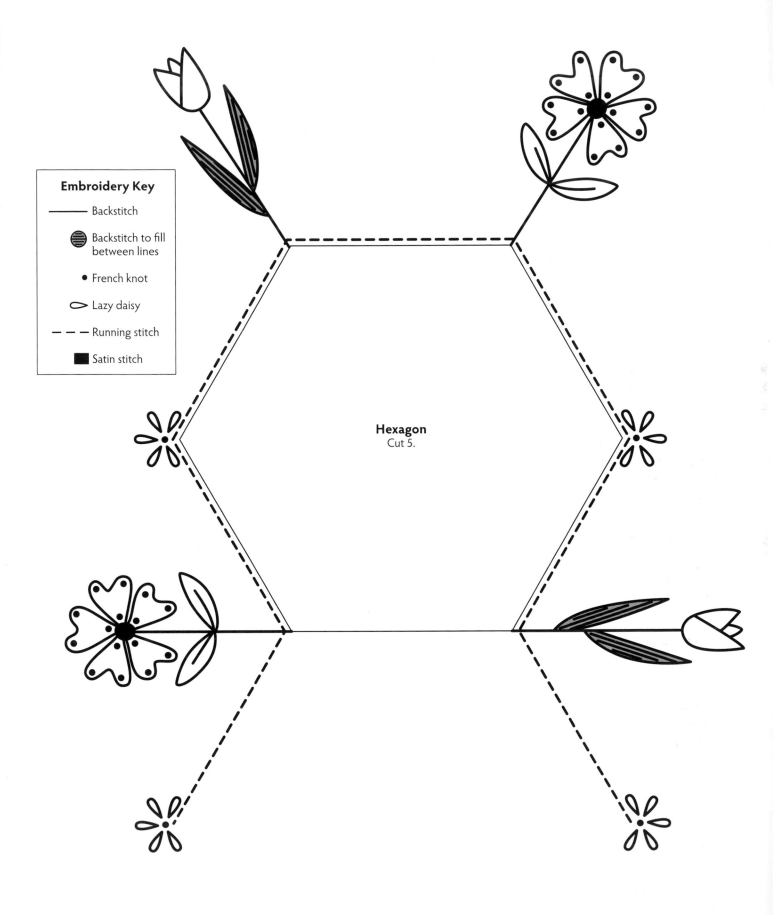

Embroidery Key

—— Backstitch

Backstitch to fill between lines

• French knot

Lazy daisy

‑ ‑ ‑ Running stitch

▪ Satin stitch

Hexagon
Cut 5.

Vintage Baskets

Stitch a pretty little topper that's just right for afternoon tea or to display all the time with a bowl of fresh fruit or flowers.

> ✕ **FINISHED TABLE TOPPER: 30½" × 30½"** ✕

Materials

Yardage is based on 42"-wide fabric.

- ✖ ¾ yard of cream tone on tone for embroidery background
- ✖ ½ yard of blue print for border
- ✖ ⅓ yard of red print for binding
- ✖ 1 yard of fabric for backing
- ✖ 35" × 35" square of batting
- ✖ 1 skein *each* of 6-strand variegated embroidery floss in brown, pink, blue, yellow, red, purple, olive green, medium green, and blue green
- ✖ Ecru pearl cotton, size 8, for quilting
- ✖ ¾ yard of lightweight fusible interfacing, 26" to 28" wide, for stabilizing embroidery
- ✖ 3½ yards of ¾"-wide cream lace
- ✖ Brown Pigma pen
- ✖ Appliqué or quilter's glue

Cutting

All measurements include ¼" seam allowances.

From the cream tone on tone, cut:
1 strip, 25" × 42"; crosscut into 1 square, 25" × 25"

From the lightweight fusible interfacing, cut:
1 square, 25" × 25"

From the blue print, cut:
4 strips, 3½" × 42"; crosscut into:
    2 strips, 3½" × 24½"
    2 strips, 3½" × 30½"

From the red print, cut:
4 strips, 2½" × 42"

Embroidering the Designs

1. Fold the cream square in half diagonally in both directions and finger-press the folds. In each corner, trace the embroidery design onto the right side of the fabric using the Pigma pen and the pattern (page 32) and aligning the center of the design with the pressed lines. The bottom of the baskets should be about 2" up from the corners. Fuse the interfacing square onto the back of the traced square. Machine baste around the perimeter, ⅛" from the outer edges.

2. Using two strands of floss, embroider the designs following the embroidery key and referring to the photo on page 28. Press.

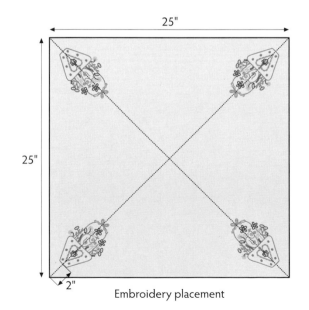

25"

25"

2"

Embroidery placement

Assembling the Table Topper

Press seam allowances in the directions indicated by the arrows.

1. Trim the embroidered square to 24½" × 24½", centering the designs.

2. Sew the blue 3½" × 24½" strips to opposite sides of the embroidered square. Sew the blue 3½" × 30½" strips to the top and bottom edges. The topper should measure 30½" square.

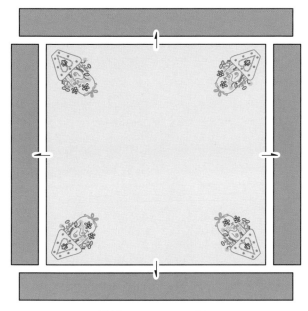

Table-topper assembly

× *Made to Measure* ×

This 30"-square table topper fits perfectly on a small drop-leaf table, giving the flexibility to use it when the table leaves are up or down. If the size isn't right for your table, adjust the size that you cut the center square (and the length of the border strips too). The corner motifs allow extra space to modify the topper and make it your own!

Quilting and Finishing

1. Layer the topper top, batting, and backing; baste. Machine quilt the cream center using a meandering design. Using the ecru pearl cotton and big-stitch quilting (page 46), quilt a wavy line through the middle of the border.

2. Cut four 31"-long pieces of lace. Place the lace ⅛" from the raw edges around the perimeter, with the scallops facing inward, and glue baste in place.

⅛"

Glue baste.

3. Use the red 2½"-wide strips to make double-fold binding and then attach the binding to the table topper (page 47).

× *Easy Does It Lace* ×

To make sure the lace shows evenly all around your topper, try this: Sew the binding to the back of the quilt and try to maintain an accurate ¼" seam allowance all around to ensure the lace scallops are a consistent depth. Then fold the binding to the front of the quilt, covering the raw edges and stitching line. This will also cover a portion of the lace, so try to make it as even as possible.

Embroidery Key

—— Backstitch

✕ Cross-stitch

● French knot

◠ Lazy daisy

- - - Running stitch

— Straight stitch

Flowers in June

Showcase favorite prints and your embroidery around the perimeter, while leaving space for a centerpiece or dessert in the middle.

✕ FINISHED TABLE TOPPER: 30½" × 30½" ✕

Materials

Yardage is based on 42"-wide fabric. Fat quarters measure 18" × 21".

* 1 fat quarter of cream tone on tone for embroidery background
* 1 square, 9" × 9", of cream-and-blue print for center block
* ½ yard of dark blue dot for center block, middle border, and binding
* ½ yard of blue stripe for pieced border and outer border
* ⅛ yard *each* of 4 assorted blue prints for pieced border
* 1 yard of fabric for backing
* 35" × 35" piece of batting
* Pearl cotton, size 12, in dark red, variegated green, light blue, and variegated dark blue
* Ecru pearl cotton, size 8, for quilting
* ½ yard of lightweight fusible interfacing, 18" to 20" wide, for stabilizing embroidery
* Brown Pigma pen
* ½" quilter's tape (optional; see page 46)

Cutting

All measurements include ¼" seam allowances.

From the cream tone on tone, cut:
4 squares, 7" × 7"

From the lightweight fusible interfacing, cut:
4 squares, 7" × 7"

From the cream-and-blue print, cut:
1 square, 8½" × 8½"

From the dark blue dot, cut:
4 strips, 2½" × 42"
4 strips, 1½" × 42"; crosscut into:
    2 strips, 1½" × 24½"
    2 strips, 1½" × 22½"
    2 strips, 1½" × 10½"
    2 strips, 1½" × 8½"

From the blue stripe, cut:
4 strips, 3½" × 42"; crosscut into:
    2 strips, 3½" × 30½"
    2 strips, 3½" × 24½"
    4 pieces, 2½" × 6½"

From *each* of the 4 assorted blue prints, cut:
1 strip, 2½" × 42"; crosscut into 4 pieces, 2½" × 6½"
    (16 total)

Embroidering the Designs

1. Fold each cream 7" square in half diagonally. Finger-press the fold to mark a placement guideline. Using the Pigma pen and the pattern (page 37), trace the flower design onto the right side of each square, placing the stem on the creased line. The stem should be ¼" from the corner. Fuse an interfacing square to the back of each marked square.

2. Using one strand of pearl cotton, embroider the designs following the embroidery key and referring to the photo on page 34.

3. Press the embroidered blocks and trim them to 6½" square.

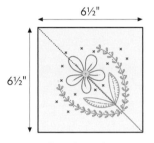

Embroidery placement

Assembling the Table Topper

Press seam allowances in the directions indicated by the arrows.

1. Sew dark blue dot 1½" × 8½" strips to opposite sides of the cream-and-blue print square. Sew dark blue dot 1½" × 10½" strips to the top and bottom edges to make the center block. The block should measure 10½" square, including seam allowances.

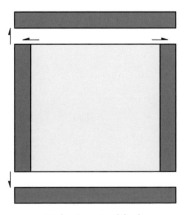

Make 1 center block,
10½" × 10½".

2. Placing the blue stripe strip in the center, join five different blue print 2½" × 6½" strips to make a side unit. Make four identical units measuring 6½" × 10½", including seam allowances.

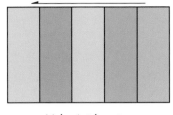

Make 4 side units,
6½" × 10½".

3. Sew side units to opposite sides of the center block. Sew an embroidered square to an end of each of the remaining side units, making sure the flowers are facing inward. Make two and sew them to the top and bottom of the center row. The topper should measure 22½" square, including seam allowances.

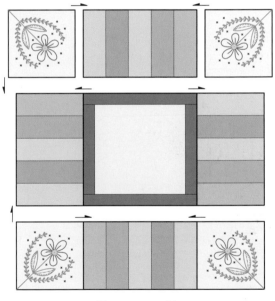

Topper assembly

4. Sew the dark blue 1½" × 22½" strips to the left and right edges of the topper. Sew the dark blue 1½" × 24½" strips to the top and bottom edges. The topper should measure 24½" square, including seam allowances.

5. Sew the blue stripe 3½" × 24½" strips to the left and right edges of the topper. Sew the blue stripe 3½" × 30½" strips to the top and bottom edges. The topper should measure 30½" square.

Quilting and Finishing

1. Layer the topper top, batting, and backing; baste. Using the ecru pearl cotton, quilter's tape, and big-stitch quilting (page 46), quilt a straight line through the middle of each dark blue border. Stitch four wavy lines in the center square, spacing the lines about 1½" apart to look like a Nine Patch. Stitch a wavy line through the middle of each blue strip and the outer border.

2. Use the dark blue 2½"-wide strips to make double-fold binding and then attach the binding to the topper (page 47).

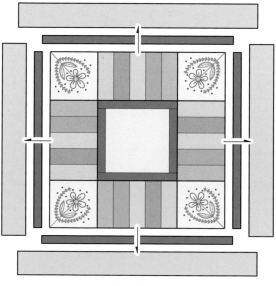

Adding borders

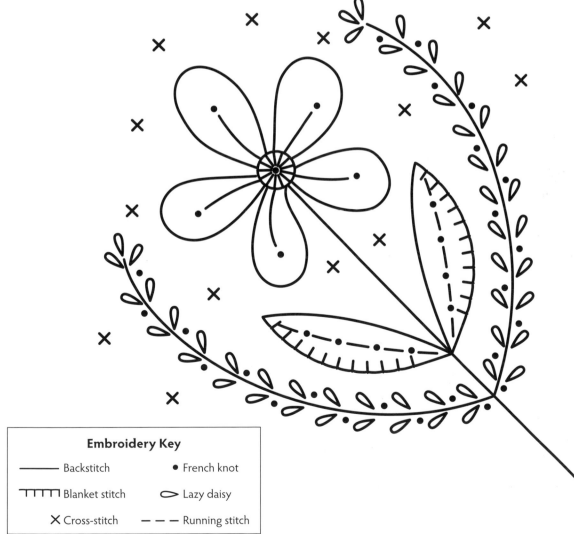

Embroidery Key

——	Backstitch	•	French knot
⊤⊤⊤⊤⊤	Blanket stitch	◠	Lazy daisy
✕	Cross-stitch	– – –	Running stitch

Floral Hexagons

Bring your garden inside with two pretty hexagon toppers. Choose your favorite motif or stitch them both for interchangeable displays.

Materials for 1 Topper

Yardage is based on 42"-wide fabric. Fat quarters measure 18" × 21".

- 1 square, 14" × 14", of cream dot for embroidery background
- 1 fat quarter of fabric for backing
- 18" × 18" square of batting
- Ecru pearl cotton, size 8, for quilting
- 1 square, 14" × 14", of lightweight fusible interfacing for stabilizing embroidery
- Brown Pigma pen
- ¼" quilter's tape (optional; see page 46)

Hollyhock Garden

- ¼ yard of purple floral for border
- ⅛ yard of green print for binding
- Pearl cotton, size 12, in variegated purple, white, variegated blue, yellow, brown, and variegated green

Daisy Garden

- ¼ yard of green print for border
- ⅛ yard of red print for binding
- 1 skein *each* of 6-strand embroidery floss in variegated green, yellow, red, and variegated light blue
- 33" of ½"-wide cream rickrack

Cutting

All measurements include ¼" seam allowances.

From the border fabric, cut:
2 strips, 3" × 42"; crosscut into 6 strips, 3" × 10"

From the binding fabric, cut:
2 strips, 1½" × 42"

Embroidering the Designs

1. Using the Pigma pen and the pattern on page 42 or 43, trace the designs including the partial hexagon outline onto the cream square. You'll need to trace the design three times, connecting the ends of the lines to make a complete hexagon. Fuse the interfacing square to the back of the marked square.

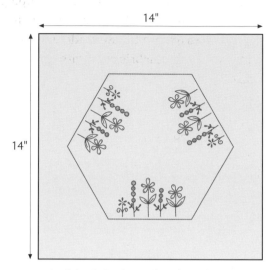

Hollyhock Garden embroidery placement

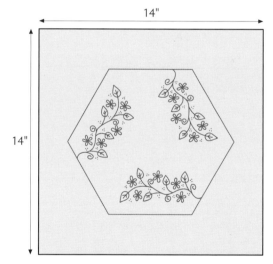

Daisy Garden embroidery placement

2. Using two strands of floss, embroider the designs following the embroidery key and referring to the photo on page 38 (Hollyhock Garden) and the photo at left (Daisy Garden).

Assembling the Table Topper

Press seam allowances in the directions indicated by the arrows.

1. Using a ruler and rotary cutter, trim the embroidered hexagon, leaving ¼" beyond the traced lines for seam allowance.

2. Sew a 3" × 10" border strip to one side, stopping about halfway from the edge of the hexagon. Press the seam allowances toward the strip. Along the top edge only, trim the excess fabric even with the edge of the hexagon.

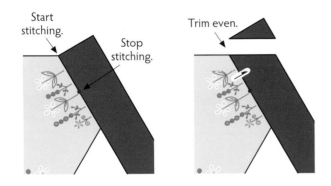

3. Working in a counterclockwise direction, continue adding the border strips around the hexagon. Then complete the partial seam. Trim the excess fabric even with the outer edges.

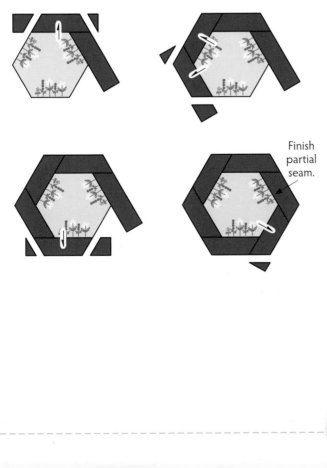

Quilting and Finishing

1. Layer the embroidered top, batting, and backing; baste. Using the ecru pearl cotton and big-stitch quilting (page 46), quilt a wavy line through the middle of the border on the Hollyhock Garden topper. For the Daisy Garden topper, use quilter's tape to stitch straight lines ¼" from the seamline. Stitch three more lines around the border, spacing the lines ½" apart.

2. On the Daisy Garden topper, draw a line ½" from the last quilted line. Cut the rickrack into six 5½" lengths. Glue a length of rickrack on the line along each side of the hexagon, overlapping in the corners. Using matching thread, sew a small running stitch underneath each rickrack scallop so that the stitching is hidden.

3. Use the 1½"-wide binding strips to make single-fold binding and then attach the binding to the topper (page 47).

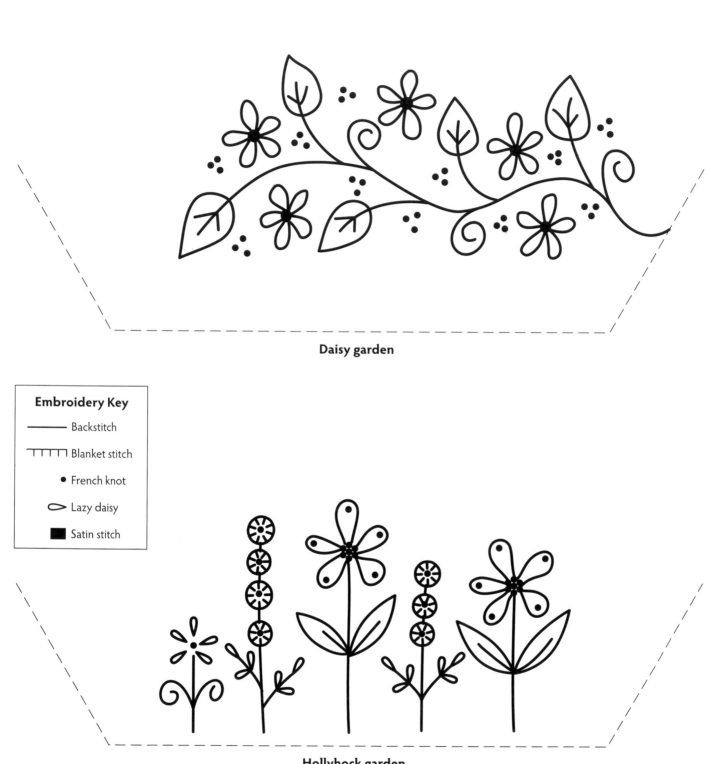

Daisy garden

Embroidery Key

——— Backstitch

⊤⊤⊤⊤⊤ Blanket stitch

• French knot

⬭ Lazy daisy

■ Satin stitch

Hollyhock garden

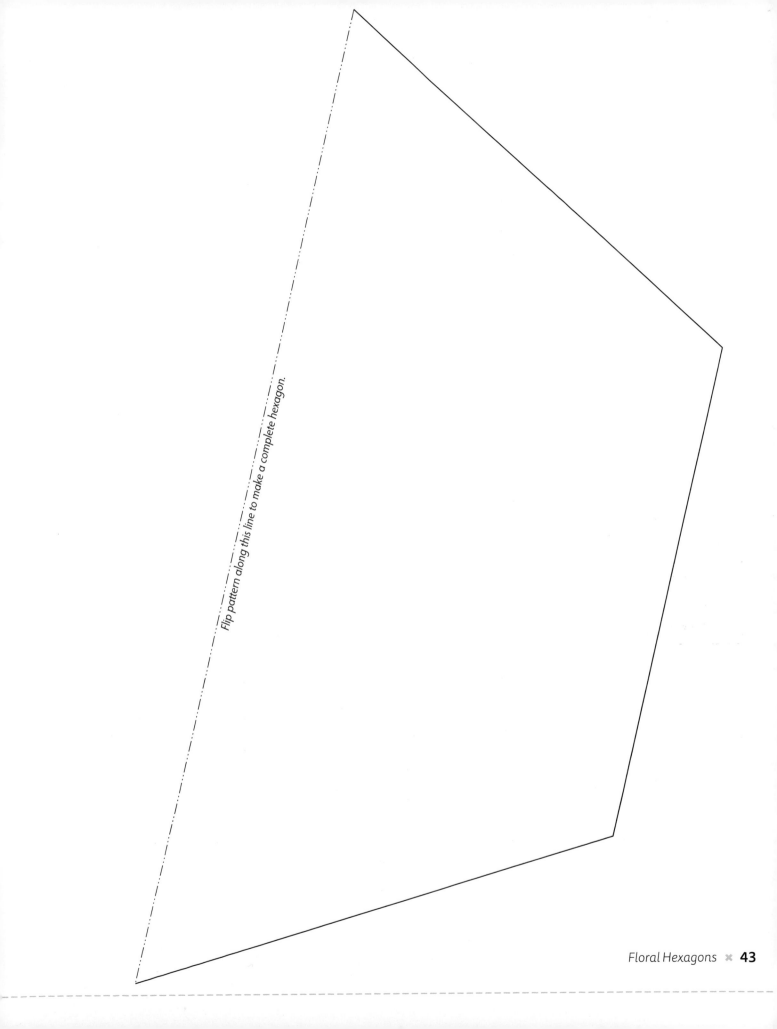

Flip pattern along this line to make a complete hexagon.

General Instructions

All the projects in this book feature hand embroidery and some also incorporate patchwork and hand quilting. In this section, I'll review some of the basics you'll need to know, but you can find additional helpful information for free at ShopMartingale.com/HowtoQuilt, where you can download illustrated how-to guides on everything from rotary cutting to binding a quilt.

Embroidery Basics

With so many different styles and techniques in the embroidery world, give yourself the gift of trying as many ways to embroider as you can. This way you'll find the stitches, threads, fabrics, and techniques that work well for you and that you enjoy the most. In this book, I'm sharing some of the simple stitches I like best, along with designs that make me happy and that I hope will bring a smile to your face.

Needles

If you've ever shopped for hand-sewing needles, you know there are many types and sizes available, each designed for a different technique. Needle packages are labeled by type, such as embroidery, quilting, and milliner's, as well as by size. The larger the size number, the smaller the needle (a size 1 needle will be longer and thicker than a size 12 needle). For embroidery, I like to use a size 8 embroidery needle (also referred to as a crewel needle). An embroidery needle is similar to a Sharp, but it has an elongated eye designed to accommodate six-strand floss or pearl cotton. You may prefer a size 7 or 9, so try them all to find what's easiest for you to use. For appliqué, I use a size 10 straw needle (also called a milliner's or appliqué needle), but a size 9 or 11 may be your preference. When hand quilting with size 8 pearl cotton, I prefer a size 7 or 8 embroidery needle. This allows me to thread the needle easily. Test a few needles until you find one that suits you.

Threads

I like to use a variety of threads. Sometimes I select threads to match the fabrics I plan to use; other times I pick a thread first, and then choose appropriate fabrics. Six-strand embroidery floss is the most common floss used. It needs to be split into individual strands before stitching since only two or three strands are used at once. I prefer using two strands and that's what I used for most of the projects in this book. Some threads, such as size 12 pearl cotton, can be used straight off the spool or ball. I always knot my thread when embroidering.

To begin embroidering, thread your needle with the appropriate floss and make a knot at the end of the strand. When you have about 4" to 5" of floss left, or when you've completed stitching, insert the needle so it's on the back of the embroidery. Then, wrap the thread around the needle and push the resulting knot close to the back of the stitch you've just finished.

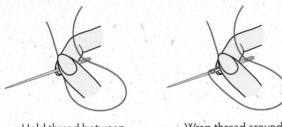

Hold thread between thumb and forefinger.

Wrap thread around needle three times.

Pull needle through wraps.

When it comes to embroidery, my favorite threads are six-strand embroidery floss from Cottage Garden Threads, DMC, Weeks Dye Works, and the Gentle Arts sampler threads; plus size 12 pearl cotton from Valdani. My favorite thread for quilting is DMC size 8 pearl cotton. I've used some of these threads in the projects in this book. Try a variety of threads and pick your favorites.

Tracing the Design

To trace or transfer the embroidery design onto your fabric, I recommend using a light box. If you embroider often, it's worth the investment. Tape the design in place on the light box, and then center the fabric on top of the design and secure it in place. If you don't have a light box, you can tape the design

to a window or use a glass-topped table with a lamp underneath.

Use a brown fine-point Pigma pen to trace lightly over the design. A fine-point washable marker, a ceramic pencil (such as Sewline), or a mechanical or wooden pencil with a fine, hard lead will also work. I always trace the minimum. For instance, if you're tracing lazy daisy stitches (loops on the embroidery pattern), only mark a dot where you will start the stitch. Leave dotted lines (running stitches) untraced, stitching where they appear by referring to the illustration or photo. Trace only the straight line for blanket stitching. You'll soon find the sort of marking that will work best for you.

I don't recommend using a FriXion pen because the marks will disappear when you fuse the interfacing to the back of the fabric after tracing.

Embroidery Fabric and Interfacing

For easier tracing, choose a light-colored fabric for the background. It's nice to use a subtle print, such as a small polka dot; the print will add some interest. Tone-on-tone fabrics also work well.

I always back the traced fabric with a very lightweight fusible interfacing. This serves to prevent show-through of the embroidery threads and knots. And, because the interfacing stiffens the fabric a bit, there is less distortion of the fabric and stitches when the embroidered piece is hooped. To do this, cut a piece of interfacing the same size and shape as your background fabric and, following the manufacturer's instructions, fuse it in place after you've traced the design and before you start stitching.

Hoops

I use an embroidery hoop to keep the fabric taut, but not tight, while stitching. Hoops are available in wood, metal, and plastic, with different mechanisms for keeping the fabric taut. Any type of hoop is fine, so take the time to find one you're comfortable with. A 4" hoop is my preferred size, but you may prefer a 5" or 6" hoop. Remember to always remove your fabric from the hoop when you've finished stitching for the day; this lets the fibers relax.

Embroidery Stitches

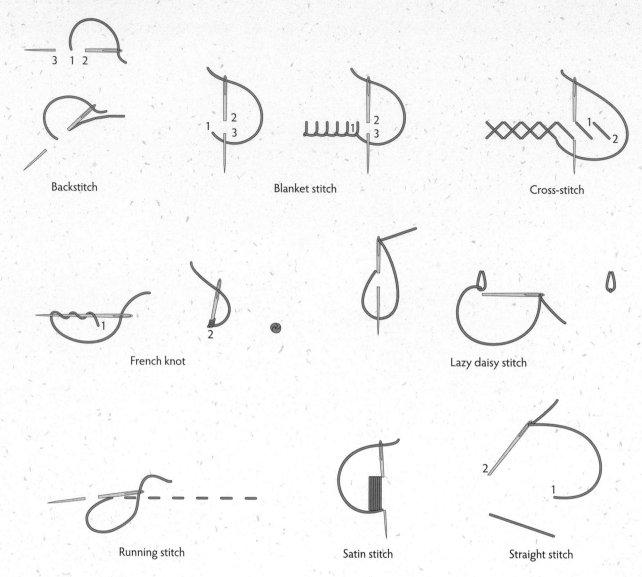

Backstitch

Blanket stitch

Cross-stitch

French knot

Lazy daisy stitch

Running stitch

Satin stitch

Straight stitch

Sewing and Quilting Basics

Please read through the instructions carefully before starting. For all projects, the yardage is based on 42"-wide fabric, the seam allowances are always ¼", and I usually press the seam allowances away from the embroidered fabric and toward the darker fabrics.

Batting

I like to use cotton batting in all my quilts. For smaller projects, such as Dainty Doilies (page 15) and Floral Hexagons (page 39), use a lightweight batting.

Big-Stitch Quilting

To add a little dimension to my projects, I hand quilt them using big-stitch quilting and size 8 pearl cotton. For straight-line quilting, I use ¼" or ½" quilter's tape. Stitching along the outer edge of the tape ensures a quilting line that's even and an exact distance from the seam. Quilter's tape comes on a roll and is both inexpensive and repositionable. For "wavy"-line quilting, freehand the quilting as you stitch. Uneven waves are cute and quirky! I also like to combine machine quilting and hand quilting; for an example, see Floral Hexagons (page 39).

1. Position quilter's tape so that one side adjoins a seamline or other feature of the project, such as an embroidered circle.

2. Thread your needle with pearl cotton, inserting the end straight off the ball. Cut a length of thread about 15" long. Knot one end with a single knot.

3. Insert the needle through the backing fabric to the front, where you want to start. Pull the backing fabric away from the batting and pull on the thread. Tug gently so the knot pops into the layers.

4. Insert the needle back into the quilt right next to the tape and approximately ¼" from the spot where your needle came up, and then bring it up through the quilt top right next to the quilter's tape. This will make a big stitch approximately ¼" long.

5. Continue in this manner until you have 4" to 5" of thread left.

6. Take the thread to the back, knot it, and then insert the needle back into the quilt in the same hole where the thread came out; pull the knot between the backing and the batting. Bring the needle out approximately 1" away. Trim the thread close to the backing fabric.

Double-Fold Binding

For larger projects, such as Flowers in June (page 33), I use 2½"-wide fabric strips to make double-fold binding. Before binding the edges (but after the quilting is complete), trim the excess batting and backing even with the quilt top.

1. Cut the number of strips listed for binding in the pattern, and then sew the strips together end to end. Press the seam allowances open.

2. Fold over one end of the strip at a 45° angle to form the start, and then fold the strip in half lengthwise, wrong sides together.

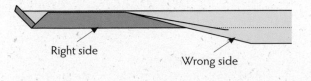

Right side

Wrong side

3. Place the starting end of the binding on the front of the quilt, at least 8" from a corner and with the raw edges of the quilt and the folded strip aligned. Begin to sew the binding to the quilt a few inches from the folded end of the binding.

4. Continue to stitch the binding to the quilt, mitering the corners as you go. When you're a few inches from the start, trim the end of your strip to the length needed to tuck it into the folded end of the strip beginning. Fold the beginning end of the strip over the tucked-in end, and aligning raw edges, sew the last few inches of the binding to the quilt.

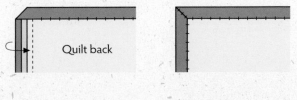

5. Fold the binding over to the back and slip-stitch it in place.

Single-Fold Binding

For smaller projects, such as Floral Hexagons (page 39), a wide, double-fold binding is too bulky, so I use single-fold binding instead.

1. Cut fabric strips 1½" wide. Stitch the strips together and press the seam allowances open as for double-fold binding. Press under ¼" along one long edge to form a fold. (This edge will be turned to the back of the quilt and sewn in place once the binding is attached to the front.)

2. Fold over ¼" at one end. Sew the raw edge of the binding to the quilt as for double-fold binding. When you get back to the beginning, trim the binding strip so that it overlaps the folded start by ¼" to ½". Continue sewing over the lapped binding until you've reached the stitching at the beginning.

3. Fold the binding to the back of the quilt and slip-stitch the pressed edge of the binding in place.

Quilt back

About the Author

I live on the outskirts of Melbourne, at the foot of the beautiful Dandenong Ranges (a series of low, verdant mountain ranges) in Australia. Growing up in a home where crafting and sewing were an important part of life, it was only natural that I tried every craft there was! To this day, I always have some kind of project in the works, from knitting to cross-stitch.

When my kids were little, I made their clothes, and when they got too old for that, I moved to patchwork. My design business was born out of a habit of always changing whatever pattern I was working on until it became a new design altogether. In 2003, some friends who were opening their own patchwork business encouraged me to design and release my own patterns. I've been designing ever since. I've also branched out into designing fabric, which is so much fun!

I teach all over the world and get great satisfaction and enjoyment from sharing my love of needle and thread. I have met some amazing women whom I now call friends. I hope to count you among them. Happy stitching!